Itty Bitty Animals

ITTY BITTY MICE

By Jay Moose

Gareth Stevens Publishing

Please visit our website, www.garethstevens.com. For a free color catalog of all our high-quality books, call toll free 1-800-542-2595 or fax 1-877-542-2596.

Library of Congress Cataloging-in-Publication Data

Moose, Jay.
Itty bitty mice / by Jay Moose.
p. cm. — (Itty bitty animals)
Includes index.
ISBN 978-1-4339-9892-8 (pbk.)
ISBN 978-1-4339-9893-5 (6-pack)
ISBN 978-1-4339-9890-4 (library binding)
1. Mice — Juvenile literature. I. Title.
QL737.R6 M66 2014
599.353—dc23

First Edition

Published in 2014 by
Gareth Stevens Publishing
111 East 14th Street, Suite 349
New York, NY 10003

Editor: Ryan Nagelhout
Designer: Nicholas Domiano

Photo credits: Cover, p. 1 Stockbyte/Thinkstock.com; pp. 5, 7, 11, 19, 23, 24 (nest, tail) iStockphoto/Thinkstock.com; p. 9 Dr. Morley Read/Shutterstock.com; p. 13 © iStockphoto.com/karlbarrett; pp. 15, 24 (pup) Chris Lishman/Flickr/Getty Images; pp. 17, 24 Kirsanov Valeriy Vladimirovich/Shutterstock.com; p. 19 Richard Boll/Photographer's Choice/Getty Images; p. 21 Digital Vision/Thinkstock.com.

Printed in the United States of America

CPSIA compliance information: Batch #CW14GS: For further information contact Gareth Stevens, New York, New York at 1-800-542-2595.

Contents

Mice are tiny animals!

They have a long tail.

They move around a lot at night.

They live in nests.

Mother mice take care of their babies.

Baby mice
are called pups.

The babies are often pink. They don't have any hair yet!

Some mice can be kept as pets!

Wild mice are not wanted inside houses. These are called pests.

Mice are sometimes used for tests. They have gone to space!

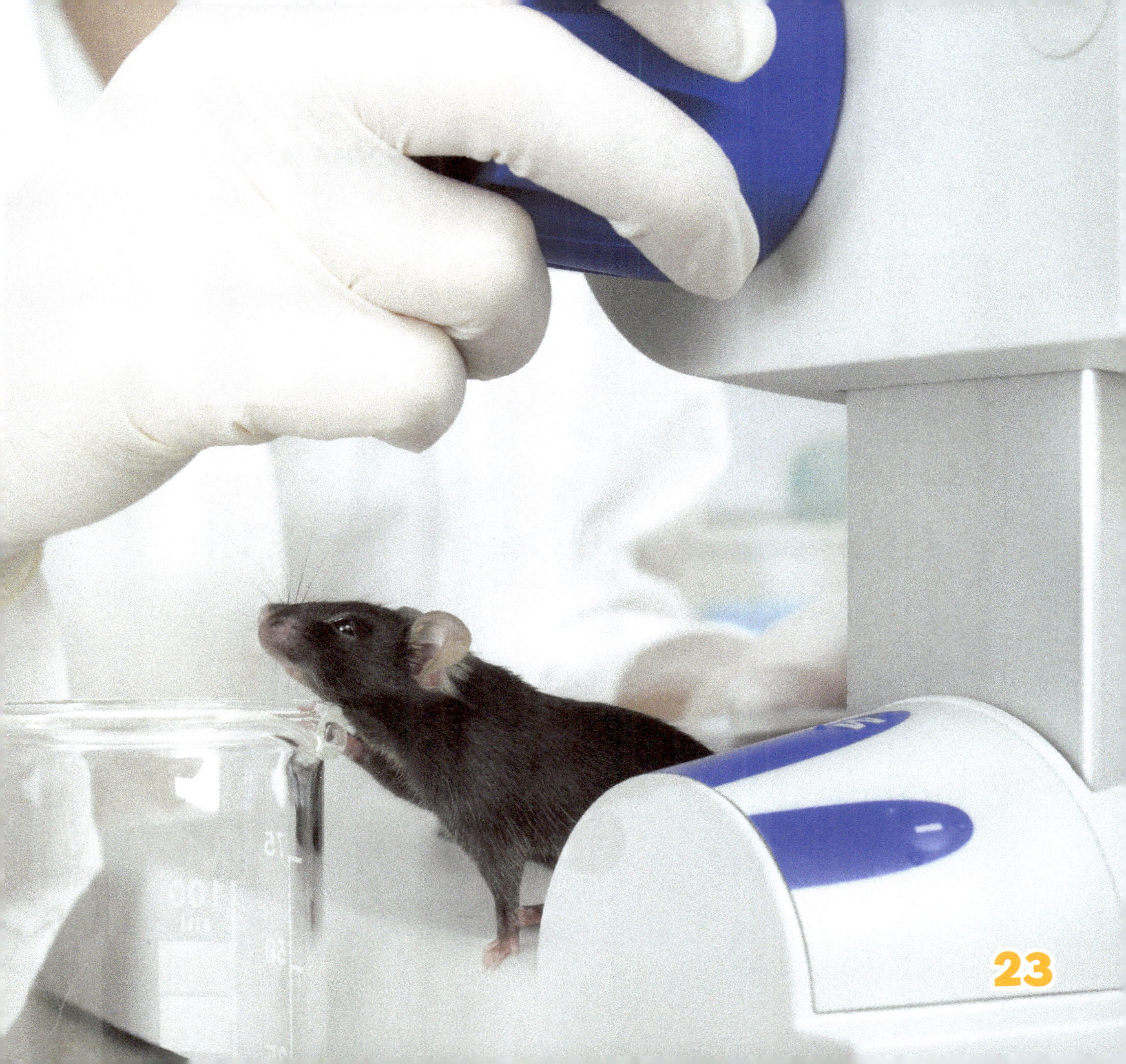

Words to Know

nest

pups

tail

Index